MW01277239

DICTIONARY OF Colorful Phrases

DICTIONARY OF
Colorful Phrases

Gibson Carothers & James Lacey

Sterling Publishing Co., Inc. New York

Library of Congress Cataloging-in-Publication Data Available

1 3 5 7 9 10 8 6 4 2

Published 1994 by Sterling Publishing Company, Inc.
387 Park Avenue South, New York, N.Y. 10016
Originally published by Sterling in 1979 as *Slanguage*

Distributed in Canada by Sterling Publishing
℅ Canadian Manda Group, P.O. Box 920, Station U
Toronto, Ontario, Canada M8Z 5P9
Distributed in Great Britain and Europe by Cassell PLC
Villiers House, 41/47 Strand, London WC2N 5JE, England
Distributed in Australia by Capricorn Link (Australia) Pty Ltd.
P.O. Box 6651, Baulkham Hills, Business Centre, NSW 2153, Australia
Manufactured in the United States of America

Sterling ISBN 0-8069-4639-3

Let's face it—we Americans are quick to adopt cleverly colorful phrases that make no literal sense. What follows is a collection of sayings commonly used and understood by Americans, but rarely found in English dictionaries. The illustrations humorously depict these Americanisms, and the stories of the actual origin of each slang expression turn out to be fascinating.

DICTIONARY OF
Colorful Phrases

Top Dog.
JAMES GIBSON

Top Dog

The precise origin of this expression is unknown, but it is theorized that the dog, long considered man's best friend, has always been viewed in a lofty position. A synonym "top banana" used to refer to the head comedian in a burlesque show, who carried a large, soft banana-shaped object which he used to hit other comedians over the head.

Far Out (or Way Out)

These expressions, which originated in the last few decades, come from baseball. A ball hit far out to left field, or right field, is difficult to catch, and fathered the phrase "way out in left field," which means well off the beaten track, and therefore, rather special.

Laugh Up Your Sleeve

A Mandarin's costumes had extremely wide sleeves which served as pockets (little Pekingese dogs were known as sleeve dogs!) and could also be used as a shield for one's face. A person who hid his face after a business deal was suspected of trying to hide a smile of pleasure at having put something over on the other person.

Quickie

Something that is made fast, and generally quite sloppily. The word originated in Hollywood in the early movie days, and referred to a low-budget movie that was hastily thrown together.

Sick as a Dog.

Sick as a Dog

The earliest known appearance of this expression in literature was in the 14th century. In the U.S. it appeared in print in "A List of Words from NW Arkansas" published in 1909. Dog lovers will be happy to know that there is no medical basis for this simile. According to veterinarians, dogs get no sicker than any other animal, including people.

To Hound Someone

This is a hunting term. When the hound dogs are let loose and start after their quarry, they chase after him, yip at him and worry him, never giving him a moment's rest until the hunters have caught him.

Hair of the Dog that Bit You

It is said that someone who wakes up with a hangover can cure it by taking a drink of the same alcohol he'd been drinking the night before. It is an extension of the old belief that the antidote to a dog bite is the burnt hair of the dog that bit you.

Kick the Bucket

Animals that are about to be slaughtered for food are often hung from a frame scaffold, and of course they kick out as they are lifted into position. Their legs hit part of the frame whose French name, *buchet,* is the origin of the word bucket in this Slanguage phrase for dying.

Raise Hob

In early English, a hob was a clown, or mischief maker, and to raise hob means to start trouble by making a fuss.

Raining Cats and Dogs.
JAMES GIBSON

Raining Cats and Dogs

According to Northern mythology, the cat is supposed to have a great influence on the weather. Similarly the dog was an attendant to Odin, the storm god, and is a symbol of the wind. So, if it makes sense to rain any type of animals, cats and dogs are the logical choices.

Stonewall

This word, which means to refuse to talk or answer, was greatly popularized during Watergate. Originally it was a cricket term which was used to indicate the kind of defensive play when one team concentrated on blocking the ball from their own wicket, or goal, rather than trying to gain the offensive.

The Last Straw

The final burden, problem, or bit of bad luck which brings you to the breaking point is often greeted with, "That's the last straw!" Sometimes it's expressed as, "That was the straw that broke the camel's back." This originated in the fable of the man who claimed that his camel could be trained to carry enormous weights if you went about it gradually, leading him up one straw at a time until....

The Cold Shoulder

In days gone by, when people traveled great distances on foot or horseback, it was customary to set out hot food and drink for visitors as soon as they arrived. If the guest was an unwelcome one, the host would only give him a cold shoulder of lamb or beef, left over from the last meal. This was considered a snub.

Cat's out of the Bag.

JAMES GIBSON

Cat's out of the Bag

This expression goes way back to the 8th century when Muhammad made it illegal to sell and eat pork. Pork lovers had to purchase their suckling pigs in bags under the cover of darkness. Frequently, dishonest farmers would place a cat in the bag instead of a pig. So, when the unsuspecting pork lover returned home, he was incredibly surprised when he literally let the cat out of the bag.

Con

One meaning of this word is simply a prisoner, con being short for convict. The verb "to con" means to trick or bamboozle someone into doing something for your benefit. Originally con was short for a kind of criminal known as a "confidence man," someone who posed as a legitimate business man and made crooked deals as a way of stealing money from gullible victims.

Flim-Flam

This is a specialized kind of "con game" in which a pair of crooks offer to share a great deal of money—often they claim to have found the money—with a stranger. They ask the stranger to take a few thousand dollars out of his bank "to show good faith," then switch the envelope with the real money for one filled with worthless paper. Thus the term flim-flam means a quick, fairly complicated series of events which confuses the victim and puts something over on him.

Foot the Bill

Pay the expenses for everyone by signing one's name at the foot of the bill, or the bottom line.

Cat got your Tongue?

Cat Got Your Tongue?

This extremely old expression got turned around at some point in history. Technically, it should be "do you have a cat's tongue?" because it is based on the simple fact that cats are incredibly quiet. Fortunately, the origin has nothing to do with the fact that tongue is a popular dish with cats.

Cat's Paw

This phrase, which is a name given to someone used and made to perform illegal acts by a scheming person, is another phrase which comes from one of Aesop's fables. In the fable a wily monkey who wanted to get some roasted chestnuts out of the fire without burning himself persuaded a cat to let him use her paw.

Gold Brick

In the days of the Alaska Gold Rush and the California Gold Rush, unscrupulous crooks would sell someone a real gold brick, and in wrapping it up in paper, would substitute an ordinary brick. In World War II the phrase took on a new meaning. A soldier who goofed off of an unpleasant job by managing to get someone else to do his job for him was said to be "gold bricking." A gold brick is closely related to a "Con Artist."

Free Loader

A fairly recent U.S. slang term, originally meant specifically one who loads up with free food and drink at a party. Its meaning now extends to anyone who goes along enjoying benefits at someone's expense without repaying him.

The Cat's Pajamas.

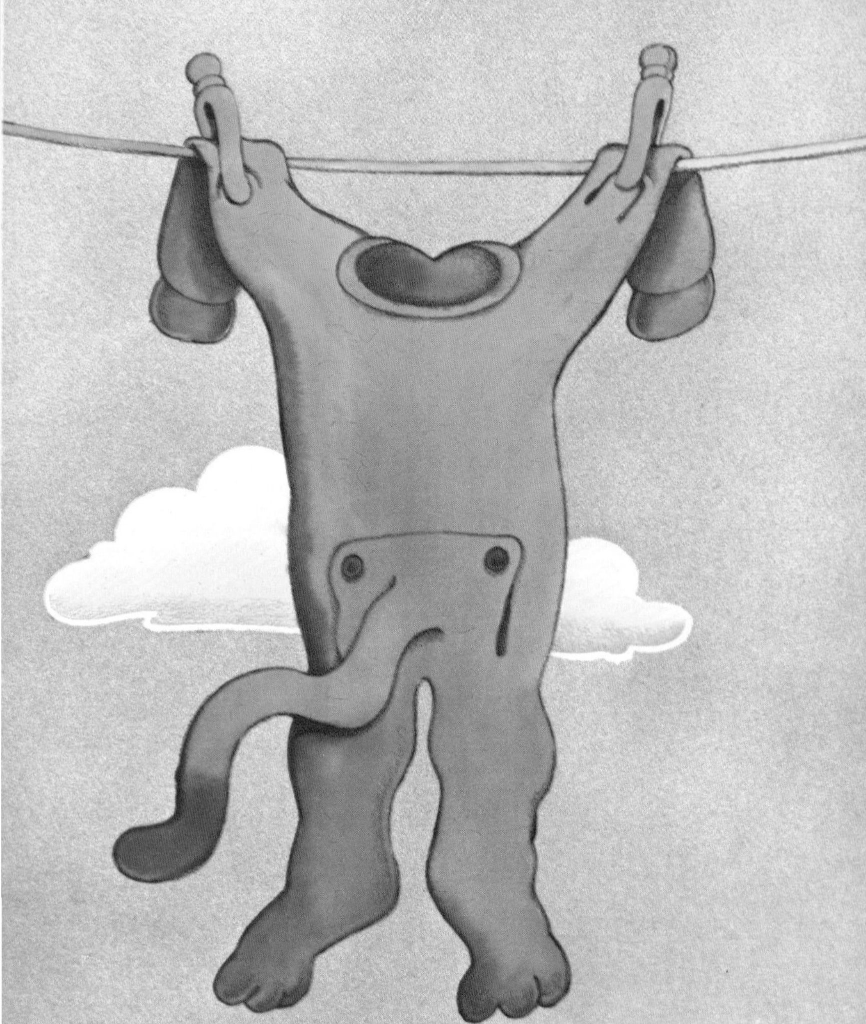

The Cat's Pajamas

This expression roared out of the 1920's along with "the cat's meow" and "the cat's whiskers." This version was most popular because in the late 1920's pajamas were still new enough to be considered daring. Clara Bow, the "It" girl of the silent screen, was frequently referred to as "the cat's pajamas."

Funnybone

There's nothing funny about a knock on the inside of the elbow which hits the funnybone. It hurts! The name funnybone is a pun on the Latin name for the upper arm bone, the humerus, but it is a nerve which crosses over the humerus close to the surface which causes the pain.

Joker

In its usual sense a joker merely means someone who plays jokes on people, but in Slanguage it means a person or a situation which can unexpectedly do an about-face, like the joker in a pack of cards, which is "wild" and can be made to represent any of the 52 cards in the deck.

Gimmick

At circuses and fairs during the 19th century a gimmick was a device used by magicians and entertainers as part of their act. Nowadays a gimmick is any tricky method for making a sale, or a business deal, often in the form of a special inducement that is unusual. The word is often used in reverse meaning by those who have exposed the trick that was meant to take them in: "The gimmick is. . . ."

Cart before the Horse.

Cart before the Horse

Variations of this expression probably go back forever because whenever there are people there are always a few clunks who do things backwards. The early Romans are known to have said "Currus bovem trahit praepostere" or "You've got the ox before the plough."

Curry Favor

This phrase, which means to seek to ingratiate yourself with someone by insincere flattery, or by doing small favors, is a corruption of the original saying, which was to "curry Favel." Favel was the name of a horse in a satirical 14th century French play. The horse symbolized evil, and the characters in the play curried him in order to soothe him and ward off trouble.

Dark Horse

This is a racing term meaning someone who is unknown—and therefore not one of the "favorites"—but may or may not have potential winning power. Sometimes unscrupulous people dyed a champion horse and passed it off as an unknown in order to make money by betting on it.

Pumpernickel

Napoleon is said to have invented this word for a kind of dark peasant bread. Napoleon liked fine white bread, but one night during one of his battles he was served a coarse, dark bread. He was annoyed, the story goes, and fed it to his horse, Nickel, instead of eating it himself, saying "This is *pain* (pronounced panh) *pour* (pronounced poor) Nickel," meaning, "Bread for Nickel."

Holy Cow!

Holy Cow!

This exclamation, which can be traced back to the early 1940's, was preceded by Holy Cats!, Holy Mackerel!, Holy Smoke! and Holy Moses!, in that order. All of these exclamations used to be considered blasphemous, but today they are primarily used by nuns and Osmonds.

Dumb Ox

As a boy, St. Thomas Aquinas had had no education when he first went to his teacher, Albertus Magnus. However, Magnus recognized the fact that his pupil was an exceptionally bright young lad and he said, "This dumb ox will one day fill the world with his moo-ing."

Crying over Spilt Milk

"Don't do it," is what we are told when we cry needlessly over something that has been broken, or lost to us, and can't be regained. The expression comes from the fable of the milkmaid who dreamed of the things she would do with the money she got when she sold her milk: Buy chickens, sell their eggs, buy something else...and eventually become wealthy. Suddenly she tripped and spilled the milk—and there went all her dreams of clothes and castles, but she decided there was no use crying over the spilt milk.

Give a Hoot

Hoot is a corruption or sound-alike for the word "iota," which is the smallest and therefore the least consequential letter in the Greek alphabet. Learned people sometimes say, "I don't give one iota."

Two Birds with One Stone.

JAMES GIBSON

Two Birds with One Stone

People have been trying to accomplish two tasks with only one effort for a long time. This proverbial expression was first recorded in 1611 from Latin. Another popular expression from the same time period is "A bird in the hand is worth two in the bush."

It's a Cinch

A cinch strap holds the saddle on a horse and the expression comes from the American Far West. When the strap is properly cinched, there is no danger of the rider coming unseated because of a loose pack saddle, or losing your belongings because of a loose saddle. Your journey will be easy. In fact, it'll be a cinch!

White Elephant

Something that costs money but does you no good—and what's more, can't be disposed of. The origin is from the country of Siam (which is the former name of Thailand) where so-called white elephants, actually very pale grey, were considered sacred. When the King of Siam wanted to punish one of his courtiers he gave him a white elephant for a present and the courtier had to keep feeding the hungry beast as long as it lived!

Odd-Ball

A term which has become popular since the 1940's for someone who acts in a bizarre, offbeat manner.

Sitting Duck.

Sitting Duck

Use of this expression began in the South during the late 1800's and increased in popularity after the invention of the shotgun and laws that made it illegal to shoot a sitting duck. This led to the similar "duck soup" which used to be considered an easy way to get rid of the evidence.

Quack

At fairs in the old days, medicine men hawked the potions and elixirs by "quacking" out in a singsong way, trying to convince people of the healing powers of their fake "cures." People nicknamed them "quacks," even though they pretended to be doctors.

Cut to the Quick

This means to hurt someone's feelings as painfully as if you had cut the sensitive area around the fingernails—the cuticle or the part underneath the nail that is known as the quick.

Make No Bones about It

The bones in this expression refer to dice, which are often carved out of bone. The phrase means to be forthright, to come out with the truth regardless of the outcome—unlike the turn of the dice, which very much affects the outcome.

Tear-Jerker

This name for a story that is so sad it "jerks" the tears right out of your eyes comes from the theatrical world in the days of melodrama.

Spring Chicken.

Spring Chicken

This expression seems to have first cropped up around 1800 in South Carolina, probably in Pamlico County, the only American county to have produced an entire book of slang words and expressions. It is based on the fact that in the old days (long before the Colonel), all chickens were hatched in the Spring.

Lay an Egg

Stage talk for a play which goes through weeks of preparation, only to fail when it opens up in the theater. It is used for any particularly striking failure where great expectations had been entertained.

Gone to Pot

This has nothing to do with a weed from Mexico. It refers to someone or something which has deteriorated badly—like leftover meat which the cook accumulates in a pot before turning it into hash.

Egg On

To egg someone on is to encourage him to keep on doing something, often something not quite nice. It has nothing to do with eggs, but is a corruption of the word "edge."

Pretzel-Bender

This expression for a peculiar person undoubtedly originated with some unknown author who was trying to dream up a really odd-ball occupation.

Turtle Doves.

JAMES GIBSON

Turtle Doves

This is an old-fashioned, unofficial name originally given to any types of dove who flew and cooed in pairs. It has been around for ages, although it has been most popularized in "The Twelve Days of Christmas." Today, it is used almost exclusively to describe lovers rather than birds.

Tie the Knot

Slanguage for getting married, this expression derived from antiquity. Tying an actual knot was part of many different marriage ceremonies. For instance, in a Hindu wedding the bridegroom tied a ribbon around the neck of his bride. Until the knot had been made fast, the father of the bride could withdraw his consent to the marriage, but afterwards, the marriage, like the symbolic knot, was insoluble.

Take the Plunge

This means to take a drastic action which can't easily be reversed, and most often means to get married. Originally the term was 19th century English racing slang. A large bet, which went deep into one's finances, was called a plunge; and of course today's Slanguage use implies that getting married is a gamble.

Hunky-Dory

An obsolete meaning of the word "hunk" is "in good condition." Tacking on "dory" makes the phrase more positive: really, really okay!

Happy as a Lark.

Happy as a Lark

The state of Nebraska gets credit for being the birthplace of this simile sometime in the early 1920's. Apparently, the expression is based on the simple fact that larks spend almost all of their time eating and singing, and are easily pleased.

Round Robin

This is a form of contest in which players compete with each of the other players until the one who is least often defeated is declared the winner. The words come from the French words meaning "round ribbon." A group of people might sign their names to a petition but wish to give equal rank to each name. So, to have no beginning and no end, they attach together the two ends of the list, which had been written on a long, narrow paper, to form a round ring.

Fit as a Fiddle

This phrase, meaning in good physical condition, probably comes from Ireland, where the fiddler at a country dance had to be in good enough shape to be able to fiddle all night long.

Blue Blood

Someone with very "noble" blood in his veins is called a blue blood. The phrase originated in Spain, where the veins of the aristocrats, lying very close to the surface under very milky-white skin, were actually said to be bluer in color than the common people who had mixtures of Moorish and other blood in their veins—or perhaps more opaque skin!

Crazy as a Loon.

Crazy as a Loon

Although this simile has been used by writers from all parts of America dating back to the mid-1800's, it appears to have originated with bird watchers in New England. It comes from the loon's call, which sounds like a madman's laugh. Alcohol and mountain fever are two of the many ways one can become this crazy, the former being the preferred.

Bats in the Belfry

If you have crazy ideas floating around in your head, people say you've got bats in your belfry. Bats are small nocturnal animals, the only mammals that truly fly, and although most varieties feed harmlessly on insects or fruits, some are blood-suckers. Even though they prey only on small animals, they can bite humans if disturbed, and may cause rabies, which drives the victim crazy—or "batty."

Blind as a Bat

Bats, being nocturnal, sleep during daylight hours and emerge at night to forage for food. If frightened out of their nests when it is bright outside, they have trouble seeing.

Paddle Your Own Canoe

This means to mind your own affairs and work things out by yourself. Abraham Lincoln was advised to paddle his own canoe by a political opponent. The word "canoe" was originally from the West Indies and meant a boat made from a hollowed log. (Ask someone to read this "French" sentence: "Pas de La Rhone que nous.")

Goose Bumps.

Goose Bumps

This term can be found in print as far back as 1867 and Bing Crosby helped popularize it on the radio in the 1940's. Synonyms include goose flesh, goose pimples and duck bumps. When a person you are with gets goose bumps, it is either because of you, or because of a draft in the room.

Gone Goose

Someone who is in a terrible fix, with no escape from his problem, is like a goose with the hunter's rifle pointing at him.

Goose Egg

A big, fat zero. The "O" is shaped like an egg, and the goose's egg is larger than the chicken's.

Egghead

This term for an intellectual, or someone with superior intelligence, is consistent with the old saying about bald men that "Grass doesn't grow on a busy street." The expression became popular in 1952 when Adlai E. Stevenson ran for President. Mr. Stevenson had a high-domed, egg-shaped bald head, and was noted for being more of an intellectual than a politician.

By the Skin of Your Teeth

This really isn't a slang phrase. It comes from the Bible (Job XIX, 20) and means, of course, by the narrowest of margins.

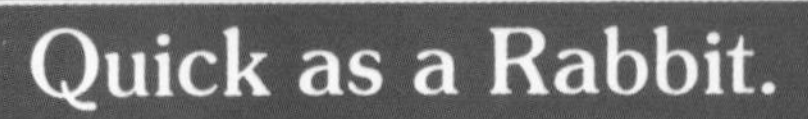

JAMES GIBSON

Quick as a Rabbit

This expression seems to have gained popularity during the mid-1800's in Texas where a slight variation was "quick as a jack rabbit." It has never been determined whether the speed refers to a rabbit's running abilities or reproductive talents.

Behind the 8-Ball

In pocket billiards a player who knocks the black ball numbered "8" (one of 15 balls, all numbered) into a pocket accidentally, automatically loses. If a player must hit a ball which is behind the 8-ball, he usually cannot help bringing disaster down on his own head.

Flash in the Pan

This phrase, meaning a spectacular beginning that leads quickly to failure, comes from the action of old flint-lock guns. Occasionally after being all primed to fire, the gun would misfire, with only a tiny flash of gunpowder in the lock-pan.

One-Upmanship

Stephen Potter invented this term in his popular 1950's book, "Gamesmanship." It means to go someone one better, to get the upper hand in a relationship by topping the other person's exploit, or by putting down the other person by forcing him into an embarrassing position.

Eager Beaver.

James Gibson

Eager Beaver

This expression originated in the Armed Forces during World War II to describe a soldier anxious to take on any task, no matter how difficult, to impress his superiors. The beaver is known to be a very busy and industrious worker.

Put the Whammy On

This expression, meaning to put a spell or curse on someone, especially by staring at him with the "whammy eye," was popularized by a character in Al Capp's comic strip, "Li'l Abner."

Bury the Hatchet

When the chiefs of western Indian tribes met together after a war to settle their differences, they buried their hatchets and other instruments of war before they sat down to smoke the pipe of peace. In this way they signified that hostilities were ended, and insured themselves that if angry words occurred, there would be no start-up of fighting among them again.

Crop Up

When something comes up unexpectedly it is said to crop up. This is a mining term which refers to an outcrop of rock containing ore which doesn't have to be hunted for because it is clearly visible on the surface.

Drunk as a Skunk.

Drunk as a Skunk

This expression first appeared in print in 1949, but similes involving intoxicated animals have been around hundreds of years and many are listed in Ben Franklin's Drinker's Dictionary published in 1737. As well as being drunk as a skunk, one can also be drunk as a goat, a boiled owl, a pig, David's sow, a herring, a loon, a mouse, or a monkey. Take your pick.

Mud in Your Eye!

It sounds pretty silly to wish someone "mud in your eye" when drinking a toast. The expression originated during World War I when soldiers (who were nicknamed "doughboys") were fighting in the muddy trenches in Europe, but evidently didn't lose their sense of humor.

To Drink a Toast

In years gone by in England it was customary to place a piece of toasted bread in one's beer to improve its flavor. That's why taking a drink to honor someone is referred to as drinking a toast.

In the Nick of Time

A few centuries ago attendance was taken at meeting by cutting a notch or nick on a wooden stick as each person entered. Someone who arrived at the last possible moment was said to have got there "in the nick of time."

Leaping Lizards!

Leaping Lizards!

The precise origin of this term is not known, but it appears to have grown up in the South during the mid-1800's and to have been based on the well-known biological fact that lizards lack the longitudinal muscles in their legs required for leaping. Thus, a lizard seen leaping should surely bring about an exclamation of shock.

Playing 'Possum

To keep very quiet or lie still in the hope that you won't be noticed is to act like the opossum which lies in a tree and pretends to be dead in order to escape being preyed upon.

By Hook or By Crook

This means to get something you want, or to accomplish something, without regard to what's right or wrong. The phrase is said to have originated in the Middle Ages when the serfs were allowed to cut wood for their fires only as high up and as far from the roads as they could reach with the hooks and crooks which they used for breaking branches off the trees.

John Hancock

If someone asks for your John Hancock, he wants your signature. Hancock was the first Founding Father to sign the Declaration of Independence. His signature, large and strong, was in the center of the document.

Busy as a Bee.

Busy as a Bee

The first known appearance of this expression in literature is 1536. There are many variations, including the Alabama version "busy as 40 bees in a tar barrel." The rigid social structure of the bee has not only given us this slang expression for being incredibly busy, but also Slanguage for someone who sits back and does very little—"queen bee."

Bee in Your Bonnet

Like the buzzing of bees in a hive, an idea can buzz around inside your head, under your bonnet, trying to buzz its way out.

Put a Flea (or Bug) in Someone's Ear

To tell someone something that will make him edgy and suspicious. Originating in the early Middle Ages, the expression comes from the kennels, where a dog with a flea in his ear acted up and seemed afraid of people.

Fly-By-Night

An untrustworthy person who is likely to disappear during the night, owing money to everyone.

Mazuma

This slang word for money dates back about five or six thousand years, and was used by Jews in Biblical times. The Chaldean word for money is m'zumon.

Timid as a Mouse.

Timid as a Mouse

This simile, like "quiet as a mouse," can be found in literature as far back as the 16th century. Mice, with an average body size of three inches, are among the smallest animals, and understandably have never liked to call much attention to themselves.

Ax to Grind

Someone who pretends to argue on purely logical grounds, but really has secret, selfish reasons for wanting something to be done a certain way, is said to have an ax to grind. Benjamin Franklin started this expression in his story of the man who asked Ben to show him how the grindstone worked. He handed Ben an ax he had brought with him, and then pretended not to understand exactly how it worked until Ben had illustrated so often, the man's ax was thoroughly sharpened!

Pan Out

This phrase from the Gold Rush days in California and Alaska means to work out well. It referred to a method of finding gold called "placer mining" in which the gold seeker placed gravel from the bed of a shallow river in gold territory in a flat pan of water. He swirled it around quickly and if there were any gold nuggets, no matter how small, they would sink to the bottom, since gold is a heavy metal. After the worthless gravel had been thrown off, the gold "panned out."

Fly in the Ointment.

Fly in the Ointment

This figure of speech first appears in the Bible in the first verse of the tenth chapter of Ecclesiastes. It's based on the fact that even though a fly is small and insignificant, it can make its presence felt in a major way...like when it lands in your soup.

Dyed-in-the-Wool

This phrase has come to mean genuine, a true friend, one who could be trusted to stick with you. If wool yarn is dyed before it is woven into cloth, the dye will penetrate completely, and the color will last, whereas if the cloth is woven before it is dipped into the dye, it will only color the surface and, as the cloth becomes worn, the color will disappear.

Back to the Salt Mines

In Czarist Russia prisoners were often banished to the dreary wastes of Siberia and sentenced to work in the salt mines there. The phrase means to get back to work and start toiling again.

Hammer and Tongs

To go at it "hammer and tongs" means to work as hard and fast as a blacksmith, who holds the red-hot horseshoe—or whatever he is forging—on his anvil with a pair of tongs, and then hammers away as hard as he can, working as quickly as possible before the metal cools.

Fish out of Water.

Fish out of Water

This simile dates back to at least the 14th century where it appears in Chaucer's prologue to the "Canterbury Tales." It has always been used to describe a situation when a person is out of his element—unprepared. It is still extremely popular all over America, even though fish might actually be better off out of the water in some of our polluted rivers and streams.

Hard-Hat

Modern safety regulations for workers, especially those in the construction trades, require them to wear a melon-shaped hat made of metal to protect them from possible falling or flying objects. Thus the term has been extended to include the workers who have strenuous outdoor occupations.

Hard-Nose

In early United States carnival slang this term was used to refer to a skeptical, suspicious person who questioned the tricks or illusions of the performers. Hence, someone who is hard to convince.

Jerkwater Town

In the United States, this means a town so small and unimportant that trains stopped there, during the last century, only to take on water or "jerk" water for their steam engines from overhead tanks which were placed at intervals along the railroad tracks.

Hook, Line & Sinker.

JAMES GIBSON

Hook, Line and Sinker

This expression appears to have originated on the Maine coast in the late 1800's. Originally, it referred to an over-zealous fish, but today it refers to a person who swallows another person's line of talk. A synonym with less romantic overtones is "whole hog."

Fish or Cut Bait

There is no place for a lazy fisherman in a fishing boat, so you must cut bait for others if you're not going to fish. It's easy to see how this applies in other situations.

Mealy-Mouth

The derivation of this word is Greek and it originally meant honey-mouth. It is used to describe a person who uses sweet, honeyed words hypocritically in order to curry favor with someone.

Moonlighting

In America today this means to hold down a second job, usually at night. But in Ireland at a troubled time in its history it referred to acts of agrarian violence and vandalism committed at night.

Higher than a Kite.

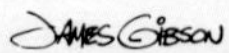

Higher than a Kite

This expression rose to popularity around the turn of the 20th century in the New England area, primarily in Maine. It is synonymous with "sky-high." Originally, both of these similes referred to someone who was very happy and excited. Today, it can also refer to someone who is under the influence.

Go Fly a Kite

The words are meaningless, but the expression is easily understood to mean "get lost." The verb "to kite" means to falsely raise the amount written on a check, as for instance by placing a 1 in front of 14, raising it to 114. Perhaps the phrase originally meant to get rid of someone by sending him off to do a finicky, difficult job.

M.C. (Master of Ceremonies)

That was the name of an Officer appointed by James I of England whose job it was to make certain that proper formalities were observed at fancy balls and feasts where decorum might be forgotten. The present-day "M.C."as he is often called is in charge of seeing that the entertainment is pleasing to the guests.

Right-Hand Man

This expression for a person's principal helper goes back to the days of knights. A knight's bodyguard would stand at his master's right, so that his own right hand would be free to use the sword if necessary to defend his master.

The Pits.

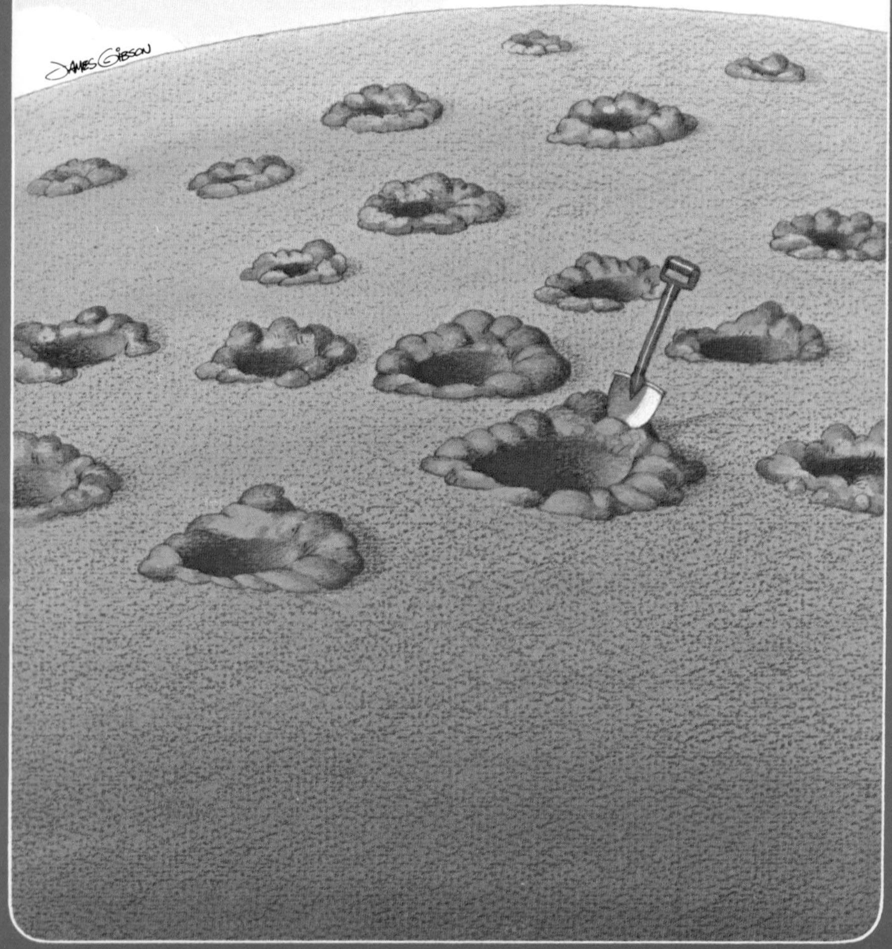

The Pits

There is no information currently available on the origin of this relatively new slang expression meaning lowest of the low. However, the leading theory is that it was first used in the late 1960's to describe a New York subway car during rush hour.

Down in the Dumps

This phrase, meaning low in spirits, has several possible origins. It might mean that one feels he is down in the pit where the garbage is dumped. Perhaps it originated with the word damp, not the one meaning moist, but as in "to damp down a fire." By depriving the fire of fresh air one makes it burn more slowly and last longer, but of course it gives out less light and heat.

Cold War

This phrase originated after World War II when many issues were still unsettled and everyone was tense and worried. It means a warlike situation without actual fighting.

Get Cracking

This means just about the opposite of cracking up, or falling apart. In Shakespeare's day a crack was a bright, keen person, and to get cracking means to get started with all your wits about you.

Shooting the Breeze.

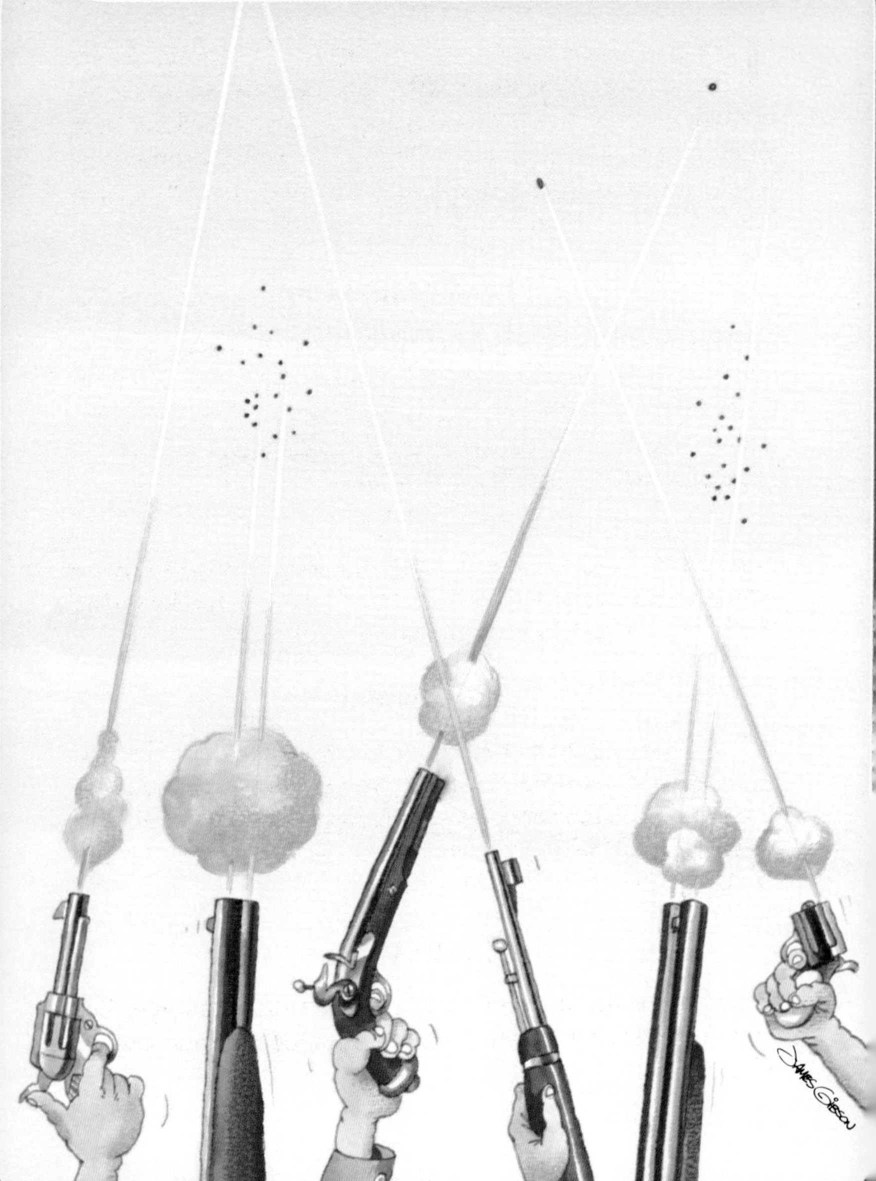

JAMES GIBSON

Shooting the Breeze

This expression, meaning talking without purpose, can be found in print in the 1920's, but did not gain national popularity until the 1940's. There is some debate over whether it originated in the military or on college campuses. A similar expression, although frowned upon by the S.P.C.A., is "shooting the bull."

Shoot Your Bolt

This means to make a great try at something, unsuccessfully, and have no further resources. In the old days, archers using a crossbow had only one bolt to shoot, unlike the bow-and-arrow archer, who had a quiver full of arrows.

On the Beam

Modern air terminal towers send out radio beams to guide planes as they approach the airport. A plane that is following the beam accurately is on the correct path.

Up to Scratch

In the 1800's when a prizefighter was knocked down he had 8 seconds to get up and walk across the prize ring to toe a line that had been scratched in the dirt floor. If he could not "toe the line," he lost the fight, because he couldn't "come up to scratch."

Strike Oil

Even before the acquisition of oil, a natural resource, became of critical importance, striking oil meant happening on a lucky find.

Fork in the Road.

JAMES GIBSON

Fork in the Road

This expression is probably about as old as roads. It first appeared in print in the U.S. around 1750 and seems to have always enjoyed greater popularity in the South, especially Georgia and Arkansas. By the way, there is also a "knife in the road," but the closest thing to a "spoon in the road" is a dip.

Fork Out

A finger was called a fork in Old English thieves' slang, so to fork out meant to hand over money or whatever, using your fingers.

Pin Money

This is money, generally a very small amount, which a housewife sets aside to make small purchases for herself. It is separate from the household money, and she can spend it as she pleases, perhaps for frivolous purchases. The term started a few hundred years ago when pins and needles were not only costly items, but difficult to come by, and money was set aside to buy them when the itinerant merchant showed up.

Break a Leg

Believe it or not, this isn't a mild form of "drop dead." It actually means "Good Luck," and was invented by actors, who are very superstitious and believe it would bring them bad luck to receive good wishes for opening night!

Slow as Molasses.

Slow as Molasses

This simile can be traced back to the early 1900's in New England where the complete expression used to be "slow as molasses in January." When people finally realized that molasses was not too swift at any time during the year, today's abbreviated version took over.

Sour Grapes

When you fail to get something that you really want, and say, "I didn't want it, anyway," that's called "sour grapes." The expression originated about 2000 years ago in the fable about the fox and the grapes written by the Greek slave, Aesop. The fox smelled some delicious wild grapes growing on a vine wrapped around a tree, but when he found that they were out of his reach, he said, "They were probably sour."

Red-Letter Day

A lucky or happy day is often referred to as a Red-Letter Day because all medieval calendars, which were handwritten by monks living in monasteries, had feast days and holidays (holy-days) penned in red ink instead of black.

Apple-Pie Order

This expression originated in France and is an English corruption of the phrase *nappe plié,* meaning neatly folded linen or table napkins. Anyway, the term is applied to things that are methodically arranged, even if it originally had nothing to do with apple pies.

Breaking the Ice.

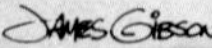

Breaking the Ice

This comes from the maritime necessity of one ship breaking up the ice on rivers and channels to allow for the passage of other ships in winter. The present meaning seems to have blossomed in Victorian times when it was a lot harder than today for members of the opposite sex to "break the ice."

The Hot Seat

To be in this uncomfortable spot means that you have to come up with a really good—and immediate—solution for the trouble you're in. It refers to the electric chair on which the death sentence of a condemned prisoner is sometimes carried out.

Moot Case

Also known as a "moot question," this phrase goes back to Anglo-Saxon days in England. The town hall where questions of government were decided was usually called Moot Hall and therefore the phrase means a question which is open to debate, or not worth debating.

Dingbat

Any little object that can be tossed easily is a dingbat, a doodad, doohickey or thingamajig.

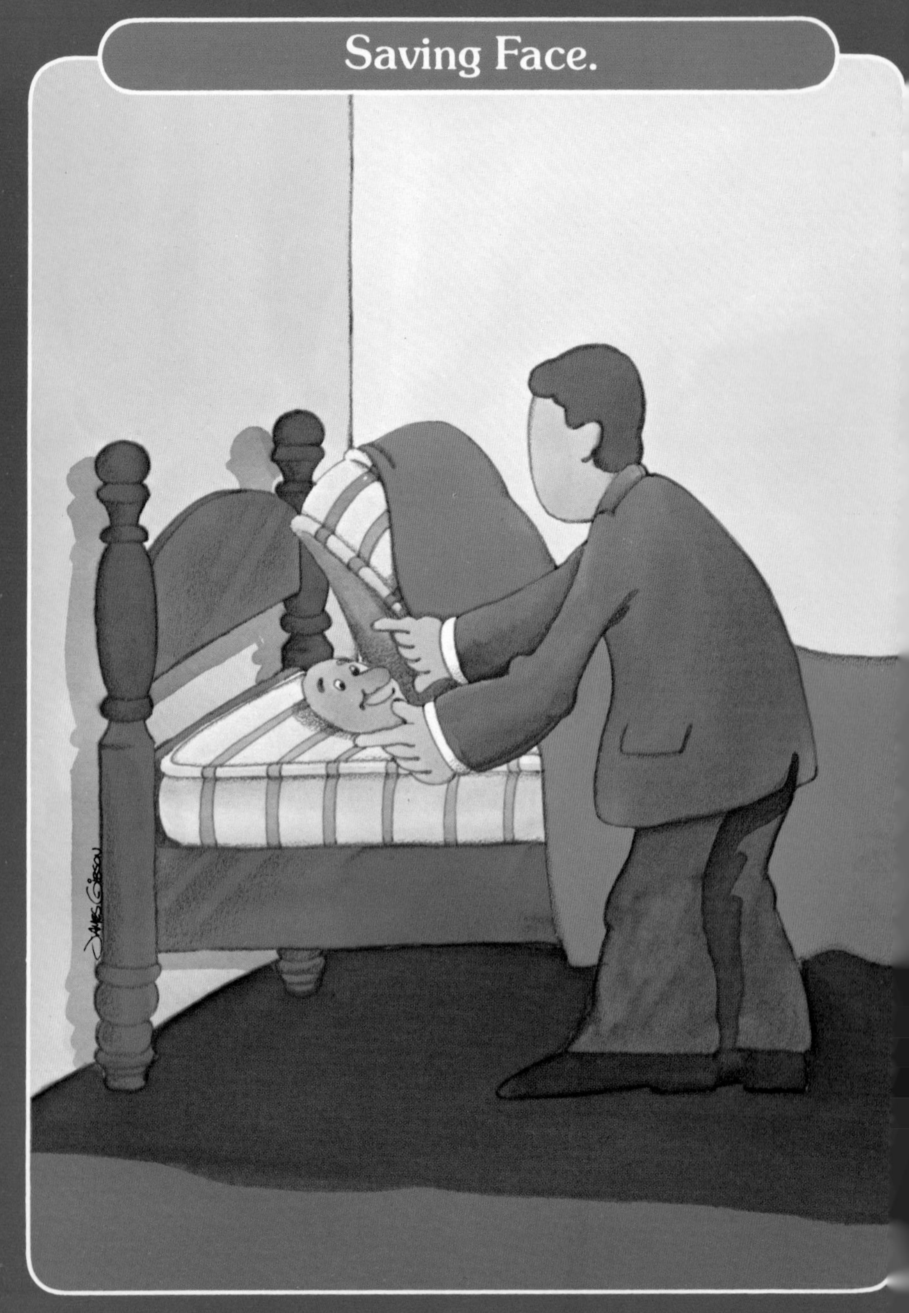
Saving Face.

Saving Face

This expression was originally used by the English community in China to describe the many devices the Chinese used to avoid incurring or inflicting disgrace. The exact expression does not appear in Chinese, but "to lose face" and "for the sake of one's face" are common.

Ugly American

This phrase has come to mean exactly the opposite of its original meaning. Applied to a tourist, the Ugly American means a person who is loud, boastful and not very polite to the people whose country he is visiting. In the book by that name written by William Lederer and Eugene Burdick, the main character was a fine man who did a great deal of good for the foreign people he lived among, but who just happened to have a rather ugly face!

Spitting Image

Probably "spitting" comes from the Anglo-Saxon word *spittan.* A "speaking" likeness is what is meant. In the South, people say "he is the very spit and image of his father" and this probably is derived from "spirit."

Fuzz

Slanguage for cop or "the law," this name was derived from the nickname for the FBI or the Federal Narcotics Bureau, namely, the "Feds."

Lead Balloon.

Lead Balloon

This relatively new American slang term meaning a flop, arrived on the scene around 1950. Synonyms include "bombed" and "laid an egg," both of which also reached popularity heights during the 1950's. One might easily conclude that the "fabulous fifties" had their share of flops.

The Heat's On

This is American underworld slang indicating that the gang, or the wrongdoers, were being put under considerable pressure by police investigations into their affairs. By extension (at least in TV police dramas) policemen are referred to as "heat."

Red Herring

This derives from a longer expression—"neither fish nor flesh, nor good red herring"—used by John Heywood in the 16th century to describe a woman. An actual red herring, dried, salted and smoked to get its red color, was used in fox hunting. It was dragged across a fox's trail to destroy the scent and lead the dogs to follow a false trail, making it more difficult for the hunters.

Willy-Nilly

Literally, willy-nilly is the Americanization of "will I, nil I" with nil standing for the negative.

Icing on the Cake.

Icing on the Cake

As one might expect, this expression gained popularity in America during the depression years when one was considered lucky just to get a plain cake. An expression with the same meaning comes from another course in the meal—"anything more is gravy."

Pie in the Sky

This phrase means false promises of wonderful things to come—at some future time! It originated about 1905 in America when union organizers warned workers not to believe the promises of management, because "You only get pie in the sky when you die."

Eat Humble Pie

After the huntsmen, in days gone by, brought in fresh-killed deer, the lords and ladies feasted on roast venison, while the servants were given the poorest parts of the animal, the entrails, heart, liver and other innards, baked in a pie. The innards were known as "'umbles," so the people who didn't count for much ate 'Umble Pie.

Cheesecake

During a time when women's dresses hid most of their legs, a newspaper photo of a woman posed in such a way that her legs were exposed was called cheesecake, possibly because of the old photographer's trick of getting his subject to smile while saying, "Cheese." The cake, of course, is something everyone loves.

Under the Weather.

H

L

JAMES GIBSON

Under the Weather

This expression began to appear frequently in print during the 1850's, notably in a Herman Melville novel published in 1857. It comes from the fact that seasick sailors were allowed to go below decks to get out of the high winds and rains of a storm. The term took on more figurative than literal meaning with the invention of the airplane.

Hep

This is soldier Slanguage from way back in the beginning of the 20th century. When foot soldiers were being trained to march, the drill master would count "*hep*, two, three, four," etc. The soldiers who stepped in rhythm and hit "hep" in the right sequence were in step, and therefore they were "hep."

Zany

Not new, zany is an Italian word. The *zanni* was a clown who played the part of a buffoon on the Italian stage. Starting in the 16th century the word was applied to any simpleton or bumbling fool.

Tongue in Cheek

If you keep your tongue in your cheek you can't speak clearly, so you are deliberately telling a "white" lie, or one of slight importance. The term began in the middle of the 19th century.

Flying Colors.

PINK
YELLOW
GREEN
RED
VIOLET

JAMES GIBSON

Flying Colors

This is an old maritime expression that can be traced back to the 17th century. The allusion is to a victorious fleet of ships sailing into their home port with their flags flying triumphantly on the mastheads.

Be Leery

The archaic meaning of leery is alert in looking for trouble. It came to mean being so suspicious and wary of a person or a situation that you're afraid of it.

Lower the Boom

This expression means to suddenly stop a situation from continuing, or perhaps to prevent someone from doing what he is contemplating. The boom on a sailing ship is a heavy horizontal spar which holds the lower edge of the sail in position while it is raised. When it is suddenly lowered, if it hits a man, it stops him dead in his tracks.

Take the Wind Out of Your Sails

In a race between two sailboats, if one captain can maneuver to come alongside his opponent on the windward side, his sails will prevent the wind from getting to the sails of the other boat. Immediately the other boat's sails will flap and the boat will lose headway and begin to flounder helplessly, quite a letdown for the sailors who had been sailing smartly along just the moment before!

Tip of the Iceberg.

Tip of the Iceberg

The origin of this expression is much like its definition—very little of it is known. Only about ⅛ of an iceberg appears above the surface. As one might expect, the term is traced back to the men who first sailed the ships in the waters near the Arctic Circle.

Pigeon English

Whether it's spelled "pidgeon" or "pidgin," this expression has nothing to do with birds. It is what the traders in China called the dialect spoken by the natives attempting to talk English. The Chinese had difficulty saying many "r" and "l" sounds and also the word "business"—it came out sounding something like "pigeon" and that is how this *lingua franca* came to be known. That is the French term meaning "the language of the Franks" who were doing business in the Moslem world in the Middle Ages.

Crying Towel

A chronic complainer was thrown a crying towel during World War II. However, this idea may have come from the boxing ring custom of having a fighter's manager throw in a towel when his man had had enough.

Cool One's Heels

This expression comes from the horse and carriage days when a horse's hoofs got so heated during a journey that the coach had to stop while the horse "cooled his heels."

Pass the Hat.

Pass the Hat

Entertainers and religious reformers spawned this expression back in the mid-1800's by using their hat to collect money. This procedure in turn helped create other hat terms such as "talking through your hat," "hat in hand," and "old hat." Obviously, these entertainers and reformers didn't always get rave reviews.

Big-Wig

In Europe in the 18th century, men of quality wore powdered wigs. Some wigs were small and didn't even cover the wearer's hair, but important men such as judges, high church officers and noblemen wore large, long wigs which came well down over their collars. They were called big-wigs after their hairpieces, which distinguished them from less important people.

High Mucky Muck

This comes from the Chinook Indians of Alaska. "Hiu muckamuck" means "plenty of food," and a person who eats plenty must be wealthy and important. Today the term is applied mostly to people who throw their weight around and think they are more important than they are.

Make One's Mark

Literally this phrase means to "sign" your name by making a mark on the paper because of being unable to write. It has come to mean to make a success of your life, especially if you have started out humbly (like an illiterate person).

In a Pickle.

In a Pickle

This expression goes back four or five hundred years to the Dutch saying, "in de pekel zitten," which means to literally sit in the salt liquor used for preserving vegetables—an uncomfortable predicament to say the very least. Shakespeare helped heighten its popularity when in *The Tempest* he wrote "How cam'st thou in this pickle?"

Panic Button

This term came into use during the Cold War which followed World War II, but first let's look at the word panic, which has an interesting origin. It comes from the Greek god, Pan, a mischievous little fellow who liked to frighten people by playing his pipes suddenly, in the dark of night, causing the hearer to jump with fright even though there was nothing scary to be seen. After World War II there was supposed to be a special button in the White House which the President could press to call out the bombers and battleships if he panicked and thought the Russians were about to attack. Nowadays to press the panic button means to go into a frenzy of worry.

Black Eye

Used figuratively this expression means a damaged reputation. A real black eye indicates that a person has not only been undignified enough to get into a fist fight, but has probably lost as well, so to give someone a black eye has come to mean telling something discreditable about him.

Raisin' Hell.

Raisin' Hell

Believe it or not, this term is attributed to a woman in Kansas back in the late 1800's. Mrs. Mary Ellen Lease is given credit for the slogan "Kansas should raise more hell and less corn!"

Cornball

Meaning overly sentimental, rather silly and unsophisticated. A cornball statement or action is what you would expect from a rustic person, a farmer type, from the American agricultural states known as the "corn belt."

From Pillar to Post

There are two versions of the origin of this phrase, which is most often used in the expression "being hounded from pillar to post," meaning chased back and forth. Some say that it comes from the early days of tennis, a game that goes back to the 13th century, and referred to the ball being tossed back and forth. Another version suggests that the words stand for pillory and whipping post, punishments which were meted out to luckless offenders in olden days.

Gung-ho

A Slanguage adjective for a person who is zealous or ambitious beyond the call of duty. The term began during World War II, as a rallying cry of the Marines on Guadalcanal in the Pacific. In Chinese it means "work together."

JAMES GIBSON

Face the Music

It is generally believed that this expression was first used to describe an actor's fear as he came on stage before his audience, thus facing an orchestra in the pit below the footlights. However, some historians believe it to have a military origin, referring to a dishonorable discharge when a soldier used to be literally "drummed out of camp."

Go-Man-Go

This musicians' term originated about 40 years ago as a term of encouragement by members of the band for the soloist producing a prolonged, difficult passage on his drums, horn, etc.

Offbeat

A term for unconventional, unusual behavior which probably originated in jazz musicians' slang for someone whose rhythm varied from the beat being followed by the rest of the band.

Freebies

In the 1950's this expression came about, originally meaning a free meal, or a free ticket to a show or sporting event, and now meaning simply, "at no cost."

Twofer

A sort of a version of a freebie, a twofer was originally a sales device started during the Depression to keep Broadway shows alive. Special tickets were issued which allowed the holder to buy two tickets for the price of one: "Two-fer one."

Index

The authors and publisher wish to acknowledge the assistance given them by Peggy A. Boehm.